THREE PINT TURN

THREE PINT TURN

And other breath-taking tales

NEIL KELLY

Cartoons by Martin Honeysett

MICHAEL O'MARA
BOOKS LIMITED

First published in Great Britain in 1986
by Michael O'Mara Books Ltd.,
20 Queen Anne Street,
London W1N 9FB.

Typeset by SX Composing Ltd.

Printed and bound by L. Rex Offset Printing Company Limited

ISBN 0 948 397 31 4

ENOUGH TO TAKE YOUR BREATH AWAY

Although this book is full of anecdotes and cartoons about the subject, drinking and driving is no joking matter. In Britain alone, according to a judge's recent summing up, drunken drivers kill or maim a hundred people every day. That's nearly 40,000 every year, and the latest figures reveal that 35% of all drivers killed were over the legal limit.

Sadly most driver's don't seem to care.

One in four of them now regularly drives while over the limit and among the 18-34 age group the proportion is as high as one in three. They all believe they can handle their drink.

Research has shown, however, that if you drive when just slightly over the limit you are seven times more likely to have an accident. Double the limit and you're thirty times more likely to harm yourself or some innocent third party.

In the United States 27,000 people died last year thanks to drunken drivers. That's considerably more than were killed by hand guns. But at least in the States, legislation and public pressure are doing something to curb the problem. Here, many still regard the drinking driver with a degree of sympathy. "After all, there but for the grace of God, go I."

Last year a record 250,000 breath tests were carried out on Britain's roads, and over one million in France. God's grace is becoming less merciful, as the numerous people who drunkenly drove their way into this book will testify. In retrospect they make for amusing reading. At the time they were potentially lethal.

And that's serious.

B DAY

At midnight on October 8, 1967, Britain was invaded by one million breathalysers. It was a sobering thought for the country's motorists. No longer would they have to try and walk straight along a chalk line or attempt to clearly recite, 'Truly Rural' or, 'The Leith Police Dismisses Us.' From that night onwards they would be required to blow into the bag.

The outcry was deafening. Hot air blew everywhere.

A. J. P. Taylor wrote in the Sunday Express that its introduction was, "enslaving man to a machine." A leader in Autocar boldly stated: "One cannot help being mauled about by today's legislators and planners. Under the new regulations the onus will be upon the suspected to prove his own innocence. Worse than that, he will be required to provide the evidence which might prove his guilt."

The nation's brewers were also less than enthusiastic about the arrival of "this Diabolical Device' which, they argued, would produce a £90 million slump in their sales over the first six months. The stock market agreed with their prophecy. Brewery shares tumbled as country pubs reported takings down by as much as half during the first week of the breathalyser.

One rural publican took only 4/6 (22½p) all day. "It is the most pernicious piece of anti-democratic legislation ever passed," he said joining hundreds of his colleagues in petitioning parliament.

Meanwhile an enterprising Banbury turf accountant was offering motorists a 7/6 (37½p) annual insurance policy against possible conviction. Should they end up being convicted he was prepared to pay their fine and £10 a week for their first three weeks in jail.

Thousands of other motorists were rushing out to buy their own breathalysers at the rate of 100,000 a day, or swallowing handfuls of 'neutralising pills', or even persuading their wives it was time they learned to drive.

"Now you really *can't* ask a driver to have another drink," wrote the ad-men between drinks, while on car radios up and down the country Engelbert Humperdink was smugly singing the week's number one hit: 'The Last Waltz.'

COMING OF AGE

The breathalyser is now old enough to drink. It was eighteen on October 8, 1985.

DEAD DRUNK

A 41 year old brewery salesman was banned from driving for 10 years after a court was told he was six times over the legal limit. According to a doctor who gave evidence at the trial this was not only the highest level of intoxication he had ever encountered it was also way past the lethal dosage.

In mitigation the salesman said he had only been doing his job.

"Come on, Mr Jones, make it twenty pints and you've got the job."

JUST TESTING

The first person to fail a breath test did so in May, 1967 – five months before it became law. He ended up appearing in a Dundee court.

Somewhat confused the Dundee Sheriff asked the police surgeon who had carried out the test where he had acquired the equipment.

"From a toy shop," the surgeon replied.

"Then why did you use it?" the sheriff enquired still confused.

"To familiarise myself with its use," the surgeon answered.

"So it was just a wee practice?" asked the sheriff.

The Surgeon nodded his head. The sheriff shook his head in bewilderment and dismissed the case.

COOL RESPONSE

A Sydney wit on being asked by the police to 'blow in the bag' replied, "Why, are your chips too hot?"

ALTERNATIVE TRANSPORT (i)

While standing in the dock of a Plymouth magistrates' court the defendant pointed out that if he lost his licence he would also probably lose his livelihood.

"My dear man," the magistrate benignly responded, "You should have thought about that before you committed the offence. Besides, it's a plea which over the years I have grown all too familiar with. As I've pointed out to your predecessors, driving isn't the be-all of existence. There are other ways of getting from A to B. May I remind you that this city does support an excellent public transport system . . ."

"I know, sir, but . . ." the defendant tried to interrupt.

"Please, if you'll allow me to finish," the magistrate insisted. "I myself came to this court this morning on a bus and will return home on one. It's convenient and economical and in my opinion a much under-utilised form of transport. There are too many cars in this city and people have become all too dependent on them. I'm sure you'll find the change refreshing . . .

"Yes but . . ." the defendant tried a second time.

"And think of all the money you'll save", the magistrate continued refusing to be interrupted. "Mark my words, after a couple of weeks you'll be as enthusiastic about travelling on a bus as I am." For a moment he paused and looked down at his notes. "And what precisely do you do for a living?"

"I'm a bus driver," came the reply.

ALTERNATIVE TRANSPORT (ii)

Rather than risk his licence and the lives of others for being over the limit, a Cincinnati man elected to leave his car behind and jog home.

He had almost reached his destination when he was stopped by a passing patrol car, questioned and arrested for being a roadway hazard.

"No lights, failure to indicate before a turn and not wearing a safety belt."

A ROADSIDE ATTRACTION

Many countries also allow random testing, including Australia. In Melbourne police use what has become less than affectionately known as a 'Booze Bus' to randomly stop and test suspect drunken drivers at the roadside.

Shortly after their introduction a motorist who had been over-indulging stopped next to one of his own volition. Without realising his mistake he went up to the front and demanded a ham roll and a strong coffee.

A DROP OF THE IRISH

A possibly apocryphal story tells of an Irishman seen by the Guardia driving his ancient and none-too-sturdy motor car across a ploughed field. Deciding not to risk destroying their own car one of the officers jumped out and gave chase. The Irishman on seeing this waving apparition of authority came to a hesitant halt.

"You've been drinking!" the officer accurately diagnosed on reaching the wreck of a car and smelling the over-powering fumes coming from its driver.

"Shanks to be to Jesus for that," the driver replied with relief. "I tort my shuspenshun had gone."

SWEARING WHITE IS BLACK

South Africa has its problems including, it seems, a lack of a sense of humour. Apparently, breathalyser stories only reach the papers if at least 12 people have been killed.

One who wasn't killed was driving to Pretoria when he saw a police road-block ahead. Knowing he had soaked his veins he was fairly keen not to go through it. So he stopped his car about half a mile away and moved into the passenger seat. Then he waited for the police to come to him. Which they did. Nonchalantly smoking a cigarette he told them how on seeing a road-block ahead his black driver had stopped the car and run off.

Being white they believed him.

ON SAFARI

Another story, this time from the Transvaal, tells of a driver on his way to the town of Nelspruit who crashed into a female Hippo. The beast was badly injured while the driver suffered only a swollen hip, though his car was a write-off.

After the accident the driver still shaken (and stirred) admitted to police that he had been drinking and was an alcoholic. He also said, "I've been seeing a lot of animals lately. I had no idea this was a real one."

16

"That's funny; I went straight through the pink elephant down the road."

IT PAYS TO ADVERTISE

To celebrate France's new breathalyser laws last July, Paris police mounted a massive check and stopped more than five hundred drivers passing through the Place de la Concorde. Yet not one single driver was found to be over the limit.

Amazing? Not really. For several days before, the place and time of the check was widely advertised in the press and on the radio. Better still, kindly *gendarmes* turned a blind eye when male drivers hurriedly swapped places with their wives.

FIRST BLOOD

One of the first people to fall foul of the breathalyser was a young absconder from Borstal who was arrested at fifteen minutes past midnight for being drunk while driving a taxi.

Unable to pay the fare he had decided to steal the taxi while its rightful owner had gone to phone the police.

When finally caught he was charged with absconding, resisting arrest, assaulting a police officer, driving a taxi while unfit through drink and without the owner's consent, and without a licence or insurance. He was then asked if he had anything to say.

"Any chance of a drink?" he replied.

A QUICK EXIT

Aware that he was over the limit and having been banned from driving once before, a Stepney gas-fitter chose an unusual way to avoid the breathalyser.

When he saw a police car flashing him in his rear mirror he elected to jump out of his car – despite the fact that it was travelling at 30 mph.

POLICE INTERFERENCE

Taking his case to appeal a young Canadian from British Columbia was finally acquitted after the judge was told by an expert that radio waves had interfered with the results produced by a Breath-Analysis machine.

The expert went on to state that the radio waves had come from the local Royal Canadian Mounted Police station.

PROFESSIONAL PRIDE

Philip Morgan followed the advice of his friends after a drunken dinner party. He left his car behind and went home in a mini-cab.

But as he was being raced down a London street at an alarming speed he realised the driver was in an even worse state than himself.

"Are you OK to drive?" he tentatively enquired.

"Sure," the driver confidently replied. "Besides, they never stop a mini-cab."

A few minutes later he was stopped for trying to beat a set of traffic lights in Notting Hill.

A CAPITAL IDEA?

A provincial judge in Cambridge, Ontario has come up with a drastic way of dealing with drunk drivers. After presiding over 19 cases in one morning he announced, to the horror of the first defendant in the afternoon, that offences would immediately decrease if the names of offenders were regularly taken from a hat and officials, "Stood them up against a wall and shot them!"

HORSE POWER

A fisherman, severely sloshed, entered a fish and chip shop in Kawakawa, New Zealand. Shortly afterwards he was followed by a horse.

The shop owner, initially stunned, quickly regained his composure and angrily demanded the horse be removed.

"Don't you like horses?" the fishermen slurred.

At this point the police arrived having received a report that the fisherman had earlier tried to enter a bar with his steed, and earlier still, a hotel. They joined the shop owner in insisting the horse be led out.

Confronted by so many irate people in such a small space the horse bagan to panic, while the policeman desperately tried to grab its reins and pull it out of the shop.

Eventually everyone, and the horse, were standing outside on the pavement. The shop owner demanded retribution, the police an explanation.

"Look, I'm not supposed to drink and drive, so I'm drinking and riding, OK?" said the fisherman.

The horse shook its head, issued a deafening neigh and galloped off into the night.

SKODA AND TONIC

The Soviet Union also has a breathalyser, made by Lion Laboratories – a British company. However, since officially no-one ever drinks and drives finding stories is like trying to find a smile in a Siberian salt mine. Facts, though, do occasionally surface.

Soviet citizens unfortunate enough to fail a breath test can expect to receive a hundred rouble fine and a driving ban of up to three years. Additionally, they might end up in one of the many sinister sounding 'sobering-up stations' – which may be a euphemism for a Siberian salt mine.

When asked about drinking and driving a Soviet official formally stated, and completely out of context, "that accidents involving seven to ten year old children in Latvia have decreased by 40% in the last five years."

Which is reassuring news, especially if you happen to be a Latvian child aged between seven and ten.

LIGHTING UP TIME

Next time a policeman shines a torch in your car, beware. It could be one of the new 'sniffer' torches capable of reading the level of alcohol in your breath and displaying the result on a small miniature screen in the handle.

TAKING THE PISS

A Cardiff bricklayer who failed a roadside breath test was taken to the nearest police station and given a second test which he also failed. He was then asked to give a blood or urine sample. He chose to give the latter.

But when the constable's back was turned he stole the sample and hid it inside his overcoat pocket.

It only made matters worse.

For he ended up being charged, amongst other things, for theft: the theft of urine.

LACK OF PRACTICE

A Shropshire lad from Telford succeeded in getting breath-alysed the same day he had passed his driving test.

Stopped for weaving across the road after celebrating his pass with friends at a local pub, he told police it was unfair because he wasn't yet used to drinking and driving.

"It's a great motoring school, they give you driving *and* drinking lessons."

SHANGHAI SURPRISE

Russia's neighbour, China, is an even harder place to find drink and drive stories. Even finding out whether they have a breathalyser is difficult enough. When that question was put to a man at the Chinese Embassy he enigmatically replied, "Organic or inorganic?" It transpired he thought the enquiry was about fertilizer.

The question was repeated. He said he would have to go and ask the Embassy driver. Minutes passed. He returned to announce that the driver couldn't be traced. Perhaps he'd been breathalysed and arrested?

But there is one story about a Shanghai bus driver. Fuelled with too much Tsing Tao beer he drove his crowded bus past a number of even more crowded bus stops before finally coming to a halt outside his home where he slumped over the wheel and fell asleep.

No wonder everyone rides a bike in China.

A NAMED DRIVER (i)

A Jersey man accused of drunken driving and violently resisting the police, which he denied, was not helped by his name: George Lush.

A NAMED DRIVER (ii)

The US State Department of Motor Vehicles has finally decided that booze and driving don't mix. It has therefore recalled its special licence plates: BOOZE, BOOZEMAN, BOOZEUP and BOOZERS.

BOOZER, however, has been allowed to remain because it's an individual's surname.

TOO GOOD TO BE TRUE

Several years ago Surrey police, keen to improve their image, held a campaign to encourage good driving. Officers would discretely follow cars for several miles and those drivers who obeyed every rule of the road would eventually be stopped and congratulated.

One of the drivers they stopped, however, turned out to be over the limit. That was why he had been driving so carefully.

FIREWATER

You should never mix your drinks, particularly if you're a fire-eater.

Prince Prometheus (stage name) discovered just how fiery his fuel was when he inadvertently swallowed a mouthful during his act. A powerful blend of turpentine, paraffin and Polish spirit, it measured 120% proof and placed him three times over the legal limit when he was later stopped for cutting in front of a patrol car.

GALE FORCE WIND

During the first month of the breathalyser police made the mistake of stopping a motorist outside Bradford. He was a professional wrestler, albeit a somewhat drunken one.

When they asked him to take a breath test, he put their equipment to the test by filling his lungs and then blowing the bag apart.

SMASHED!

Few people have made such a conspicuous attempt to get prosecuted for drinking and driving as Robert Long, an unemployed steel worker from Pittsburgh.

On becoming the proud owner of a second-hand Lincoln, he drove down to his local bar to show it off to his friends. Much toasting was done and many admiring glances cast in its direction. His friends unanimously agreed he had bought a fine example of American automobility.

But despite all the eulogies when the time came for Long to leave the car stubbornly refused to start.

Compliments became good-natured jeers and Long, embarrassed and several pints the fuller, became at first frustrated then furious. Cursing he finally agreed to let his colleagues bump start the car into life.

It was a short life, however. Ten minutes later, while waiting in a queue of traffic for the lights to change, the engine stalled. Once again Long's emotions quickly ran the gamut of frustration to fury as the battery died. Jumping out, he started attacking his new investment; kicking off the hub caps, wrenching off the wing mirrors and in a final fit, pulling off the front bumper.

It was then that the police arrived.

MARKED MEN

Sarasota county in Florida believes in leaving its mark. Convicted drunk drivers have a red sticker stuck to their rear bumpers which reads: CONVICTED DUI (Driving under the influence).

Furthermore, they are only permitted to use their cars to drive to and from their place of work.

"One more conviction and they're gonna take my shoes."

VARYING STAGES OF INTOXICATION

Nearly every country in the world now uses some form of breathalyser, though the limit varies widely.

In Czechoslovakia, Japan and Turkey you can't drink and drive at all. Even a shandy will in theory put you over the top.

In the United States, however, what state you're in will or won't get you banned depending upon which State you're in. In Texas it's still legal to drink and drive providing you're not drunk, while in New Jersey any host who serves too much liquor to a guest and allows him or her to drive away may be sued for damages by anyone subsequently injured. Recently a restaurant had to pay out nearly 4 million dollars in damages to the relative of a victim killed by one of its guests. In the adjacent State of New York persistent drunk drivers not only lose their licence but also their car. It's kept impounded until their ban is over.

The country with the highest limit is Swaziland. There, if you can find a car to drive, you're more likely to end up losing your mind before losing your licence. Their limit is twice that of Britain's.

A PUBLIC WARNING

A placard inside a Portsmouth pub contains a few well chosen words on the subject. 'Don't drink and drive, you'll only spill it.'

FOUR HUNDRED YEAR OLD DRUNK

When the nephew of King Fahd of Saudi Arabia was arrested in the West End for driving while under the influence he immediately used his influence and claimed diplomatic immunity. After consulting with his lawyer, however, he realised he could not make such a claim since he was not named on the diplomatic list. Undeterred, the prince decided to claim sovereign immunity. He was the first person to do so since Mary Queen of Scots. During her trial in 1586 she had tried to evoke a similar claim. That didn't do her much good either.

POSSESSION IS NINE-TENTHS OF THE LAW

A Yorkshire man found sitting in his car in a pub car park at 1.00 a.m. was slumped over the wheel with his eyes glazed and talking to himself in a slurred voice. He refused to take a breath test or provide a sample of blood or urine.

Magistrates, however, decided the man was on safe ground. He owned the pub.

PARDON ME

Don't burp while being breathalysed. A 35 year old Scot who did registered over the limit even though he had only consumed a couple of drinks.

Fortunately his doctor successfully argued tht the burp must have been responsible for such a high and concentrated reading, and that furthermore the man had a long history of heartburn, stomach-ache and wind.

BEER SHAMPOO

Policeman apparently have short hair so they can hear better.

When a Romford police inspector heard a burglar alarm ringing he went to investigate. While he was there he saw one of his constables drive past without stopping. He summoned the officer back on the radio and when he had returned gave him a lecture about the length of his hair. Had it been shorter he mignt have heard the alarm. However, the inspector soon realised that long hair wasn't the problem. Drink was. He asked the constable to take a breath test, which he failed.

Ironically, on leaving the Force the constable did follow his supervisor's advice, after a fashion. He now runs a hairdressers in Ilford.

DOUBLE ENTENDRE

The French for breathalyser is *'Ballon'*, which is somewhat unfortunate because the same word also means a glass of wine.

THE SWEET SMELL OF FAILURE

Stopped by police outside Adelaide a motorist opened his glove compartment, removed a bottle of deodorant and took a large swig in order to conceal the fact he had been drinking.

But his ploy failed for the deodorant contained 35% alcohol. The subsequent reading registered the equivalent of 15 beers.

'I'll say this for you, you're the sweetest smelling drunk
I've ever arrested.'

MITIGATING CIRCUMSTANCES

Stopped in Harrow for going round a roundabout the wrong way the driver was asked whether he had been drinking.

"Of course I have," he immediately answered. "So would you if you had my problems."

BELOW THE BELT TACTICS

Meanwhile, in that other venerable city of learning, a woman undergraduate one evening found herself being warned that she would be prosecuted for riding a bicycle while impaired by alcohol. The arresting officer went on to ask whether she had anything to say, which would be taken down and used in evidence etc. . . .

Although she was a good five feet away from the officer she loudly announced, "Please take your hand from under my skirt."

She never heard another word about the intended prosecution.

"MUST HAVE BEEN SOMETHING I ATE"

An Alice Springs driver arrested for being three times over the legal limit maintained he hadn't drunk a drop. Asked by the magistrate to explain his condition he blamed his son who had apparently marinated his steak in a bottle of rum before cooking it.

The magistrates said the circumstances were most unusual. He did however accept them and bound the defendant over on a two year good behaviour bond. He also ordered him to pay 200 dollars to charity.

A week later in Wagga Wagga a defendant offered a similar plea. He maintained he had been arrested after tucking into his aunt's wine trifle at his birthday party. But on this occasion the magistrate was less than satisfied. He adjourned the case and suggested the aunt appear in court, with her recipe.

A THREE PINT TURN

Suddenly realising he was going North up the M1 and not South as he had planned, a drunk and certified accountant decided to turn round and return to the slip road.

Driving North a policeman inside a motor patrol Range Rover couldn't believe his eyes when he saw a car ahead negotiating a turn across the three lanes of the motorway.

Northampton magistrates were equally amazed. They banned the accountant for three years for being so reckless.

WHY THE U.S. ARMY IS GETTING SOFT

Like almost every bar in the States, the U.S. army also used to have a Happy Hour. Trouble was many of them ended up getting too happy and then going for a joy ride. So the Pentagon decided to take some of their happiness away.

Now soldiers have what is officially called an Attitude Adjustment Hour. Instead of booze they're offered cut-price soft drinks, and that takes some adjusting to.

BELOW THE LEGAL LIMIT

Driving along the Pacific Highway in California a young couple, on their first date, were attempting to prove it was possible to make love at 60 mph. As a secondary experiment the driver was demonstrating that too much liquor doesn't make the libido go limp, or the steering wheel.

Meanwhile, in a highway patrol car parked off the road, a policeman was conducting his own involuntary experiment. How long can a cop sit still in a baking hot car? He was on the point of giving in when he was rewarded with the vision of a car hurtling past full of seething limbs. Turning his siren on he gave chase.

The man heard the siren and immediately panicked. Disengaging himself from his lover he put his foot down and at the first opportunity turned off the highway.

"We'll change seats. I've had too much to drink," he commanded as he brought the car to a screaming halt. His girlfriend tried to protest. "Don't argue," he insisted, "just switch."

A further experiment took place to see how quickly two partially undressed people could change seats. They managed to complete it just as the patrol car was pulling up in front.

The policeman was hot and angry. He demanded to know why they had raced off. The man lied and told him they weren't supposed to be there together. The policeman could smell alcohol on his breath. He was also pretty sure the man had been driving when they raced past, but he had to prove it.

"Would you mind turning the engine off, lady?" he asked. It seemed to take her too long to find the ignition but that was still insufficient proof. The police tried the direct approach. He asked her how old she was.

The girl blushed and hesitated before answering, but she knew eventually he would find out the truth. Lowering her head she whispered, "Fifteen."

"Fifteen!" cried the policeman victoriously. "I do believe you have to be a little older to drive in this here part of the State."

Her passenger was dumbstruck. Eventually he found his voice. "Fifteen!" he repeated in horror. "You told me you were seventeen!"

FLAT OUT

It would seem that even being in an operating theatre doesn't protect you from the breathalyser.

Recently a Bournemouth man was lying on the operating table still semi-conscious, having just had nine stitches in his head when a vague vision in blue came and hovered over him and demanded he took a breath test.

Unable to speak or move, the nozzle of the breathalyser was placed between his lips. The patient more gasped than breathed but it was still enough to produce a positive reading.

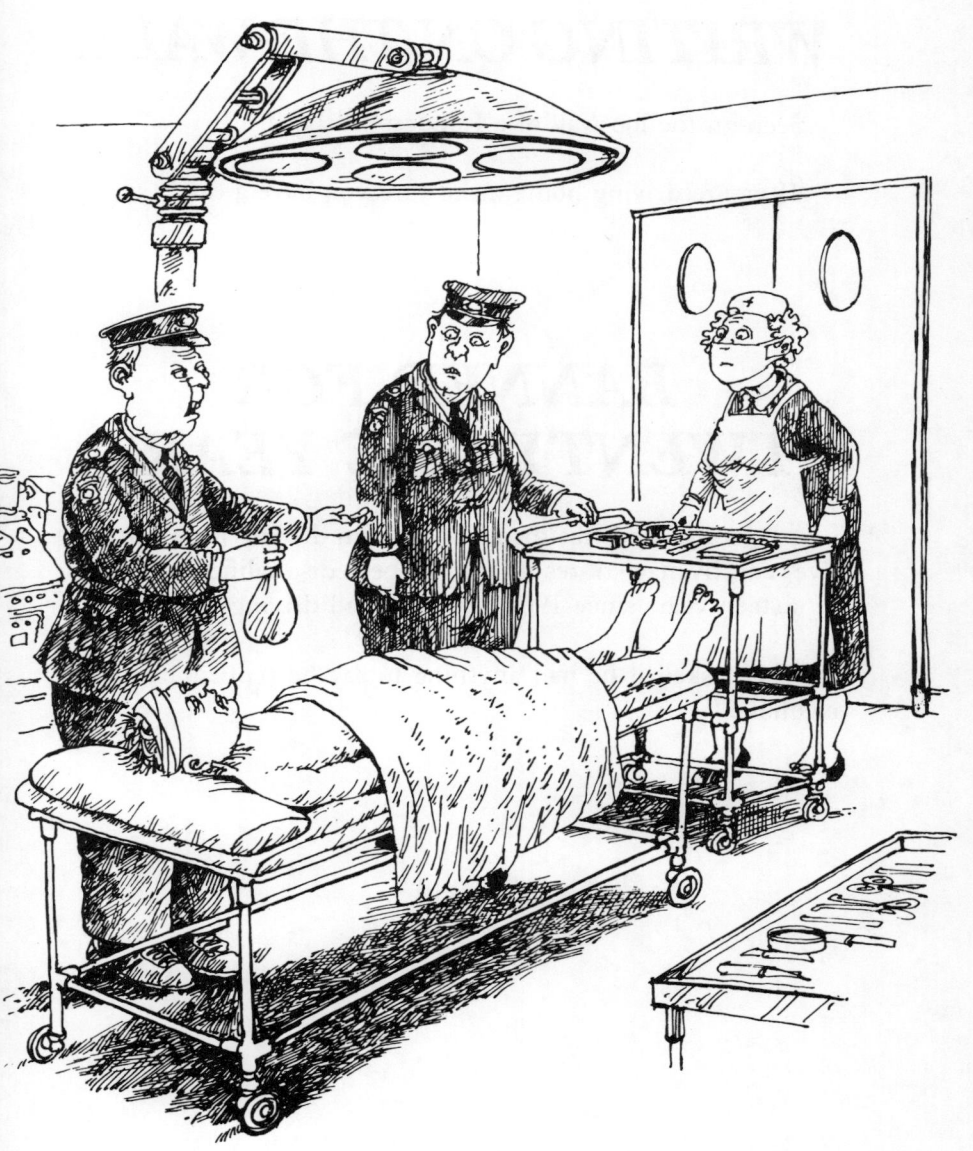

"Handcuffs."

WRITING ON THE WALL

Seen on the loo wall of a London pub:

'If you're driving home make sure you have a car.'

BANNED FOR TWENTY ONE YEARS

A motorist who was disqualified from driving for a further five years by magistrates at Hull had been disqualified for a total of sixteen years since 1962 for drink and driving offences.

When asked if he had anything to say he replied, "I'm an alcoholic."

GOING DOWN

Last Christmas a particularly unusual sentence was handed out to a young New Zealander in a Wellington Court. Having already been before the bench for several drink-driving offences the judge decided it was time to try an alternative approach. He therefore sentenced the defendant to make 30 parachute jumps after having heard his lawyer state that his client was a novice parachutist who was destroying himself with drink.

Outside the court the defendant said, "I was expecting to spend Christmas in jail, not out free-jumping from a plane every weekend. I think it sounds great.

"The judge asked me if I had jumped before as he would hate to sentence a man to parachute-jumping if he hadn't done it before and then have a death on his hands."

A DOUBLE FOR THE ROAD

Two days after he was banned for drinking and driving John Houseman returned to the police station to pick up his car.

It was not a good move.

For he had driven just three hundred yards down the road when the police spotted the same defective light that had him stopped in the first place – this time Houseman was twice over the limit.

DRUNK IN CHARGE OF A BROTHEL

A 64 year old invalid who jumped bail on charges of running a brothel in 1972 was finally caught 13 years later when he was stopped for driving his invalid carriage somewhat erratically, and breathalysed.

Although he was banned from driving for two years and fined £50 by Tottenham magistrates, no evidence was offered on the charge of running a brothel because the case papers had been lost.

DUTCH TREAT

In an attempt to curb the rise in drink and driving, the Dutch government has drastically lowered the permitted blood-alcohol level. Critics argue that it is now so low that if you merely took a deep breath as you passed the open door of a bar you would be over the limit.

HOME BUT NOT DRY

When Peter Myers finally arrived home after his annual office party he breathed a sigh of relief. Several times during the course of his journey he had thought he was going to be stopped by the police, especially as he had unwittingly driven the first part with no lights on.

Such was his relief that as he walked up the gravel path to his front door he burst into song. It was a song which came to a rapid conclusion.. As he was about to push his key in the lock, the door swung open to reveal his wife, and a uniformed policeman.

His mouth fell open in horror as his wife, a nervous type, tried to explain how she had suddenly woken up, thought she had heard a sound downstairs and phoned the police.

"This officer very kindly offered to wait for your return," he vaguely heard her add.

DRINKA PINTA

No longer do the streets of Southend ring with the sound of music as their merry milkman sang on his rounds; not since two policemen stopped his float and questioned him about his dawn chorus.

"They told me it was 7.30 a.m. and that I was making a lot of noise," he indignantly told a reporter afterwards. "I said I was singing 'The Last Waltz' and anyway it was Christmas Day. But they still insisted on making me take a breath test."

GETTING CARRIED AWAY

A solictor's clerk thought he had discovered a novel way to avoid taking a breath test by remaining in his car, locking all the doors and refusing to open his window. While the police looked on, he opened a half bottle of Scotch and proceded to drink its contents.

It got him nowhere. Or rather it got him towed away to a nearby police station where, on finally agreeing to leave his car, he was charged with refusing to take a breath test and resisting arrest.

CLASSIFIED INFORMATION

In the mid-seventies the following advertisement appeared in a Florida newspaper:

101 EXCUSES TO DRINK AND DRIVE

"Now you don't have to be lost for words when pulled in by the police.
Our unique cassette offers a host of excuses you wish you had thought of afterwards.
Play it while you drive and be prepared."

The advertisement only ran briefly before it was brought to the editor's attention and its originator, a convicted drunken driver, charged with conspiracy.

JUNGLE JUICE

Three Namibians driving a transit van through Windhock, with the radio at full volume, came to an unscheduled halt when they left the road and crashed through a shop window.

When police arrived half an hour later, the radio was still playing and the three men were dancing around the wrecked van, much to the amusement of a crowd of spectators. The police pushed their way through the crowd and attempted to stop the men from dancing. Even when the radio was turned off they continued dancing.

The three gyrating bodies were eventually forced into the back of a police van and taken to the police station. Once inside they immediately resumed their party and seemed oblivious to police questioning. Still dancing they were put in a cell.

Only in the the cold light of the following morning did one of them admit to the cause of their revelry: a lethally potent home brew, which when examined by forensics was found to contain, among other things, battery acid, drain cleaner and, to give it a real sting, scorpions!

DIPLOMATIC IMMUNITY

The ex-Panamanian Ambassador in London was regarded in diplomatic circles as being a very generous host. He was also a very considerate one for he used to keep a supply of three dozen breathalysers in his home to ensure his guests weren't over the limit.

'I think you'd better serve the breathalysers before the port, Jenkins.'

THE TEN GALLON TEXAN

A Texan tourist in his first ever trip to Europe arrived at Lisbon having consumed a substantial variety and number of duty-free toxicants during his flight across the Atlantic. Uncertainly, in every sense of the word, he set about hiring a car.

The first hire booth, ('We try harder'), politely suggested that given his delicate state he might be safer waiting until the morning. The second hire company, however, was less discriminating – both in the condition of its customers and its cars.

Having drunkenly filled in the necessary documentation, the Texan was guided out of the terminal and presented with the vision of a rusty Fiat 500.

"Is a very good car. Isa very economical," he was told by the representative. Unfortunately he was told nothing else – not even how the relic worked.

Being a large man the Texan immediately experienced considerable difficulty boarding. But eventually he managed to huff and puff himself into position even if his ample torso did touch the steering wheel. Eventually, he also succeeded in starting the car. With a rattling roar of the engine and a series of violent jerks he took off.

Twenty minutes later, close to the city centre, the Texan and the car were on the verge of the dual carriageway with smoke pouring from the boot. The smoke, heat and earlier drinks caused the Texan to sweat profusely and curse loudly. Looking up he saw a police car urgently approaching.

He was aware that he might have a problem with his alcohol consumption. However, he was totally unaware that he had driven his hired heap ten miles in first gear thinking it was an automatic.

A HOPELESS CASE

Sometimes a man can go too far, as in the case of a 38 year old electronics engineer who was seen unsteadily trying to unlock a parked car by a passing patrol car.

It turned out, however, that the car he was attempting to get into was not his. His own car, a Jaguar, was parked a hundred yards away.

When he appeared before the magistrates the chairman told him, "It is our feeling that you were so hopelessly drunk you would probably have never found your car."

He fined the engineer £5 for damaging his cell.

THE BREAST TEST

A few years ago in that 'Gomorrah of the North,' Glasgow, a young woman was seen driving off from outside a pub late at night and followed. The policeman behind soon concluded from her erratic driving that she was probably over the limit and ordered her to stop. According to the officer she immediately began flirting with him and when he asked her to take a breath test, started to provocatively unbutton her blouse. Before he could stop her, or so he said, she had exposed her breasts.

"Here. Come and give them a test," she allegedly said to him.

But in court the woman denied both the act of exposure and the remark. She did, however, admit refusing a BREATH test.

CHANGE AT THE STATION

When a Hamburg policeman stopped a woman for suspected drinking and driving he suspected something else was also wrong. For a start she was over six foot tall and her voice began to deepen once she had failed a breath test and realised she was being arrested.

His suspicions were confirmed when on arriving at the police station she went into the loo to provide a sample, and came out an embarrassed man.

TWO IS THE LIMIT

Stopped for racing up a one-way street the wrong way a Stornoway man was asked to take a breath test. The test proved negative. But the testing officer, convinced the driver was over the limit, decided the equipment must be faulty. Armed with a second device he asked for another sample.

The second test also proved negative. Despite this he was taken in a police car to Stornoway police station where, following a report by the constable, the chief inspector asked if he would take a third test.

This time the driver refused, insisting that once was enough and that he had already taken two tests.

The inspector said he appreciated the driver's co-operation so far but he suspected the officer concerned hadn't administered the test correctly. "Take a third one, just to be on the safe side," the inspector tried to enthuse.

The driver still refused and was charged with driving down a one-way street the wrong way.

ONE IN THE EYE

Asked to describe the defendant's state on being stopped the arresting officer said, "He was unsteady on his feet, his speech was slurred, his breath smelt of alcohol and his eyes were glazed."

Leaping up the defendant, a 40 year old postal worker, removed his right eye and defiantly announced, "It was bound to be glazed."

Not to be outdone the officer retorted, 'The other one was glazed too."

"And as for being unsteady on my feet ..."

BLUE BLOOD

Because he believed a motorist would lose his livelihood if banned from driving, a Newcastle police sergeant substituted his own blood for the blood test.

Unfortunately, being unaware of the switch, the motorist admitted to the doctor on duty that he had drunk seven pints of beer.

The sergeant's speculation proved right. The motorist did end up losing his job, and so did the sergeant.

VIN DE LA RUE

In the Languedoc, furious French wine growers concerned by falling sales due to the introduction of the breathalyser, took matters into their own hands. They erected warning signs ahead of police road blocks and indicated with arrows where motorists could stop for a tipple.

SWITCHING ROLLS

When a young record executive was stopped for speeding in a Rolls Royce he confessed to the police that he had always wanted to drive a Rolls and had finally succumbed to the temptation and stolen one. He was immediately arrested and taken to Hayward's Heath police station. But once there, he refused to say anything else until he had talked to his solicitor who was eventually summoned.

"Michael!" his solicitor exclaimed on seeing him. "What on earth have they got you here for?"

"Stealing a Rolls Royce."

"Stealing one? But you already have one,' his solicitor said looking puzzled.

His client moved closer and lowered his voice to a whisper. "It's the same one." He gave a smile. "You see I was somewhat over the limit and it was the best excuse I could think of at the time to divert their attention."

YOU SHOW ME YOURS AND I'LL SHOW YOU MINE

A Croydon lawyer arrested for driving while under the influence refused to give a blood sample to a doctor because the latter could not prove he was a doctor.

Appearing in court the lawyer pleaded guilty to failing to provide a laboratory specimen without a reasonable excuse.

Croydon magistrates adjourned the case for three weeks to give them time to check whether a doctor should have to prove that he is a doctor to a driver suspected of having excess alcohol in his blood.

A DIVINE RULING

George Stott believed he was blessed with divine powers. A disciple of the Renaissance mystic physician Paracelsus (who influenced Franz Mesmer) he maintained his blood contained invisible planetary forces which were able to heal the less fortunate. When arrested for drinking and driving he therefore refused to donote a specimen of his precious life force.

But the magistrates were unimpressed by either his beliefs or his excuse. They pointed out he could have provided a urine sample instead.

"That contains special powers too," Stott vainly tried to argue.

THE GREATER OF TWO EVILS

Speeding back to London on the A23 after attending the opening night of his brother-in-law's Sussex country pub, a 52 year old estate agent suddenly noticed a police car gaining on him from behind. The police car drew alongside and indicated to pull in.

Aware that he was well over the limit the estate agent felt his heart thumping as he stopped his car and awaited the inevitable.

'Good evening, sir. Were you aware of how fast you were travelling?" he heard the policeman say.

The estate agent tried to answer with his head turned away, but he knew what the next question would be. He admitted to having drunk a couple of pints.

The policeman opened a case and pulled out a breathalyser. Slowly and officially he began to explain the procedure but before he could finish he was interrupted by the roar of an approaching sports car which seconds later came hurtling round the bend with its tyres squealing.

For what seemed like an eternity the police officer stared open-mouthed at the departing Porsche. "Right!" he finally reacted. "You're damn lucky. But don't drive any further." And rushing back to his car the officer gave chase.

MAN'S BEST FRIEND

With every new piece of legislation it's never very long before people start discovering loopholes, for example where the blood sample should be taken from. A certain Hertfordshire lorry driver demanded it should be taken from his penis.

Appearing in court the doctor on duty that night said, "My immediate reaction was to comply with the request, but then I realised the foolishness of it. To have gone ahead could have had serious consequences and led to my being sued for malpractice."

The all male jury were also sympathetic. They found in favour of the lorry driver and decided that he was reasonable in offering the sample from nowhere but his penis.

"Right! That's driving under the influence and *indecent exposure!*"

KEEPING IT IN THE FAMILY (i)

When a 19 year old girl from North Shields failed the new Camic Breathalyser she had good reason to complain. Her father, Geoff McArdle, had invented it.

KEEPING IT IN THE FAMILY (ii)

An 18 year old from Palm Beach, Florida, was driving through Ohio at two in the morning when he misjudged a bend, and his station wagon left the road. Though he was not injured the vehicle was demolished. When the police arrived on the scene they discovered he had been drinking.

Just one typical case of the thousands reported every year in the US. But in this particular case the name of the 18 year old was Steven Nicklaus and the accident occurred on the road named after his golfing father: Jack Nicklaus Freeway.

NOT PLAYING CRICKET

A former West Indian cricketer who went to a police pound to collect his car ended up in a cell for 48 hours on a three year old drinking and driving charge. He was accused of not being available to receive an earlier warrant.

"It's quite incredible," the amazed cricketer said later. "They say they couldn't find me when most weekends I play cricket against them."

THE ORIGIN OF THE SPECIES

The first ever breathalyser was introduced in the USA in 1938, five years after the end of prohibition. A vast piece of equipment, it looked like something out of Frankenstein's laboratory and was aptly called the DRUNKOMETER.

NON-DRIVER BANNED FROM DRIVING

There was the case of a Maidstone man who was not a motorist, had never owned a car and had never applied for a licence to drive one. But he still ended up being prosecuted for a drink and drive offence.

The defendant, a greengrocer, told the court that having drunk about ten pints of beer he left a public house and asked for a lift home. No-one obliged. So he tried ringing a mini-cab company but due to his intoxication was unable to insert a coin in the phone box. Next he vaguely remembered scrambling into a van which rolled forward with the engine off and ran into the road where it struck a passing truck. He also vaguely recalled being arrested, regaining his senses and trying to persuade the police that he was not the driver.

After hearing his story the court ruled that if ever he did apply for a driving licence it would be immediately taken away.

A TOTAL FAILURE

The record for failing the greatest number of breath tests in the shortest period of time must surely belong to a young Southsea electrician. In three months he failed five breath tests, three of them over a four day period.

During those fateful four days he collided with a bus, got his car wedged under a row of railings, terrified a Lollipop man and finally, in trying to park his car, wrote off two others.

Pleading guilty to five drink and driving offences, as well as to four other related offences, he said that women had been the cause of his downfall.

"I've been trying to live with several at the same time," he explained. "It's driven me to drink and to the point of a nervous breakdown."

FRENCH LEAVE

After a pleasant lunch an English couple were driving their British-bought, right-hand drive Citroën a little uncertainly along one of the byways of Charente in Western France, when they were stopped by a gendarme. Automatically a breathalyser was thrust through the left-hand window.

With considerable aplomb the front seat passenger blew into it and handed it back.

The gendarme studied it, saw it was negative and waved them on.

THE GAS-POWERED MOTORIST

A prune addict, who confessed to eating two dozen every morning in order to keep himself 'regular', successfully convinced an Esher court that his over-the-limit reading on the intoximeter was not due to excessive alcohol, but due to excessive methane which had built up with all the prunes fermenting in his lower bowel.

SILENT NIGHT

A motorist's lips were sealed on the night police suspected he was over the drink-driving limit. He only stared and smiled at them as they tried unsuccessfully to obtain a blood or urine sample.

His silence saved him from being banned after magistrates at York decided he was not obliged to say anything to the police and therefore under law had not refused a sample.

The decision was based on the absence of question marks on Form 3,000 which is used by North Yorkshire police in drink-driving cases. As the defence lawyer pointed out: "If there had been question marks at the end of the statements on the form then the defendant would have been obliged to answer 'yes' or 'no'. But there were not, so he was perfectly entitled to stand there and say nothing."

LOSS OF LICENCE RESULTED IN LOSS OF MEMORY

When Fred Harris was banned from driving nothing much altered in the Harris household. The following Sunday they all climbed into his car, as they had done a thousand Sundays before, and set off for a drive in the country. But since all recently banned drivers have their car's registration number circulated to surrounding police forces it wasn't long before Mr. Harris was pulled in and arrested for driving while disqualified.

Mr. Harris was mortified and so was his family. He told the police he had completely forgotten he was banned. Force of habit had transcended recent memory. Understandably, the police found his excuse highly implausible and went ahead with their prosecution.

But Mr. Harris continued to maintain his innocence, or forgetfulness, and went to the expense of contacting a solicitor. Even the solicitor said he felt the story sounded too naive to be true and suggested his client change it. Mr. Harris refused.

Incredibly, when he appeared in court – minus his solicitor – the magistrates believed him and the case was dismissed.

ONE FOR THE ROAD

A rural landlord in Ivy Bridge, Devon, became so concerned by falling trade that he started brewing his own concoction in order to beat the breathalyser. He maintained that this elixir of sobriety when taken shortly before driving home would knock points off any subsequent breath test.

The Daily Mail was sufficiently intrigued to have the magical mixture tested, but the results were inconclusive. Nor could they persuade the inventor to provide the formula.

It will probably remain one of the great secrets of life because once the local police heard about it they warned him he would be prosecuted for a host of offences if he ever tried to serve it or revealed its ingredients.

"Personally, I'd rather be breathalysed than drink his
special concoction."

A NIGHTCAP

Not much normally happens in Harley Street at 2.30 a.m. on a cold winter's morning. That's why two policemen in a patrolling car were particularly surprised when they saw an Indian walking along the pavement in just his socks, shirt and underpants. Then they saw a second man, fully clothed, running up from behind the half-naked Indian with his arms waving and screaming, "He crashed into me."

However, the Indian seemed completely unaware of the fact and continued to walk on as if in a trance.

Getting out of his car one of the policemen walked over to the Indian. "Excuse me, sir," he announced. Still the Indian showed no reaction. In fact his eyes were firmly closed. The policeman stood in his way. The Indian crashed into him. With a start he opened his eyes.

"What's. . .what's happening?" he asked. "Where am I?" He looked around, then he looked down and saw how little he was wearing. "God!" he exclaimed with a shiver.

The other driver joined them and between pants explained how the Indian had shot out of a side street without looking and crashed into him. Then, without showing any apparent concern, he had got out of his car and walked off.

"He's been drinking too," the angry driver added. A subsequent breath test delivered the same verdict.

But when he appeared in Marylebone Magistrates Court a more charitable verdict was decided upon after it was disclosed that the Indian, who was a doctor, had drunk a small quantity of wine but then taken the drug Atvium to help him sleep.

A consultant neurological physician called to give evidence stated that such a combination could produce a state of automation, and at the time of the crash he had in effect been sleep-driving.

PROBLEM OF DRINKING AND NOT DRIVING

A recent court ruling means that people can now be convicted of refusing to take a breath test even if it turns out they haven't been drinking.

The ruling came about when a forty year old antique furniture salesman discovered that his wife's car had been stolen from outside a friend's house they were visiting. A few minutes later it was involved in a crash nearby, but the thief managed to escape before the police arrived. So when they found the salesman still in the friend's house they insisted he took a breath test, which he failed. Despite his protests he was arrested and taken to the police station where he refused to provide a second breath specimen – an offence for which he was charged.

Although the local magistrates accepted the salesman's story the police lodged an appeal and won. After the ruling the salesman said he was dumbfounded. Eventually finding his voice he added: "Although the judge said I should be found guilty he said I shouldn't lose any endorsement points or be banned and he gave me my costs."

TOO BREATHLESS TO TAKE A BREATH TEST

There are occasions when smoking can be good for you. As in the case of a 41 year old artist, and a very heavy smoker, who was arrested after police spotted her driving the wrong way down a one-way street.

She told Bow Street Court, "I'd been to a party and had about three or four glasses of red wine. I tried my best to blow into the machine but couldn't manage it."

The sergeant who arrested her said she blew into the intoximeter as if she was blowing up a balloon. "I explained to her that she should take a deep breath and blow into the machine continuously until I told her to stop. But she kept on blowing and sucking instead."

Her solicitor told the hearing, "She had a 60-a-day habit and had been smoking like that since she was 16. She failed through no fault of her own. Her best was not good enough. In fact she was so breathless the machine gave no reading."

SAFETY IN NUMBERS

Group of eminent Sydney businessmen had spent a pleasant lunch at a wine-tasting session in the Hunter Valley. On their return to Sydney in their various cars, the leading car was stopped by a patrolman and the driver breathalysed. He was found to be marginally over the limit.

"Strictly speaking," said the officer, "I should take you to Gosford police station for further testing. I suppose your friends have all been to the same lunch?"

By now all the members of the party had stopped their cars behind.

"Look, since you were all driving correctly I'll suggest this," the officer resumed. "Why don't you drive back to X (a well-known roadside stopover) and have a milkshake or two and relax for half an hour, then I'm sure you'll be perfectly fit to drive on."

And he held up the traffic while the convoy did a U-turn and drove back to have a milkshake.

THE CAR NOW LEAVING PLATFORM THREE

A Cambridge undergraduate who accepted a wager that he could drive his car along the platform of Cambridge railway station filled himself up with too much Dutch Courage and lost control at the last moment, crashing through the plate glass doors of the waiting room.

He also lost his licence for three years.

"You'll need a platform ticket for that car, sir."

POLICE PROVOCATION

The Hotel Newport on the Northern Beach part of Sydney has its players and stayers. To avoid possible testing many of them took to using an alternative route behind the hotel. The police tumbled to this and one night planted a Booze Bus in the side street.

Being cold sober, one particular local decided to learn more of the machinations of the unit. He drove past very slowly but to his annoyance he wasn't stopped. So he drove completely around the block, on to the highway and turned behind the hotel and into the side street. Again he wasn't stopped.

Seemingly obsessed with being stopped he repeated the journey a third time. The police finally pulled him in.

"I'm perfectly sober," he proudly announced.

"Pleased to hear it, sir. May I see your licence?"

It was then that he realised he hadn't got his licence with him. He was fined $30.

SITUATION COMEDY

Finding himself in court on a drink-driving charge a well-known comedian, who had better remain nameless, listened patiently while the chairman lectured him on the seriousness of the offence. Finally he asked whether the defendant had anything to say.

"Yes," the comedian replied.

"Go ahead," the chairman instructed, believing he was about to hear an apology.

"Is there anyone here who can give me a lift home?"

EASY RIDER

Encountering a motorcyclist struggling to swing a drunken leg over his bike a concerned passer-by suggested he ought to walk home.

"I can't do that," came the reply. "I need the bike to go to work in the morning. I'm a policeman.

He fell off on the first bend out of the pub car park.

DRESSED FOR THE PART (i)

Only one case appears to exist of a breathalyser being breathalysed.

It happened in Stockport where a 24 year old teacher was questioned by police after his mini-van had collided with a wall. He was on his way home from a fancy dress ball which he had attended dressed as a breathalyser.

DRESSED FOR THE PART (ii)

A Manchester arts student who went to a fancy dress party as a policeman was returning home a good few pints later when another driver cut him up. Deciding to give him a shock the student gave chase and eventually forced him to stop. But it was the student who received a shock. He had stopped a real policeman, plain clothes.

ROADSIDE CZECH

An American couple were on holiday in Slovakia when they stopped at the town of Poprad. Being lunchtime they entered a hotel restaurant in search of nourishment.

While they were waiting for their meal to arrive, the husband ordered a glass of beer. The beer came and so did a man who asked if he might join them. The man, a Czech, spoke faltering English but told the couple that his brother was living in New York. He wanted to know more about the city and listened attentively while the Americans talked over their lunch.

At the end of their meal the man wished them a pleasant holiday and the couple drove off in their rented car, but as they were leaving the city their lunchtime companion appeared standing on the side of the road next to a policeman. Raising his hand the policeman ordered them to stop. He told the husband he had reason to believe he had been drinking.

"You know I have. All one glass of it. This man saw me," the husband replied. He was at first surprised then annoyed by the man's betrayal.

"Then, please, take a test," the policeman requested. He produced a breathalyser.

"But this is ridiculous," the American protested. "There's no way I could be over the limit."

"In Czechoslovakia there is," the policeman replied with a malicious smile.

A MEAL WITH A DRINK

When police stopped a Wolverhampton man for speeding through a red light the first thing he did was to rip the road fund licence from his windscreen and eat it. The second thing he did, a little more reluctantly, was to take a breath test – which he failed.

He also failed to convince a Wolverhamapton court that he had applied for a new road fund licence several days before.

"If I was you I'd be more concerned that you're about to lose your driving licence," he was told. He was also ordered to pay £56 costs for wasting the court's time.

"Radio for another breathalyser, George, he's eaten this one."

MOTORING AIDS (i)

Police in New South Wales have called a halt to alcohol breath-testing of motorists because patrolmen feared they could catch the virus AIDS.

The police authorities said they had agreed as an interim measure to issue disposable plastic gloves and medicated cream for use when testing motorists.

MOTORING AIDS (ii)

When a Swedish motorist was stopped for drunken driving in a Stockholm suburb he told police he was suffering from AIDS and threatened to bite them unless they let him go. Growling, he was finally driven home after none of the officers would stay near him and no hospital would admit him.

MOTORING AIDS (iii)

An Oregon social worker on being stopped by police and asked to give a breath test threatened to spit on the policeman.

As he was gay the officer charged him with attempted murder.

BEGINNER'S LUCK

A motorist who was breath-tested at half past midnight on May 6, 1983 – the day the new electronic breath test was introduced – claimed the police had got their timing wrong.

The intoximeter's printout recorded the time as 11.36 p.m., not 12.36 a.m., because it was running on Greenwich Mean Time rather than British Summer Time which was one hour ahead. His defence maintained that it was therefore still only May 5 – too soon for the new law to be used.

The case was dropped.

MIDDLE EASTERN LOGIC

Another less princely, but still wealthy young citizen of Saudi Arabia living in London was also found to be over the limit when police stopped him in his Porsche. He failed to claim any kind of immunity and was subsequently banned.

A month after being banned he was stopped again. This time he was driving a Mercedes. Although not over the limit he was cautioned, via an interpreter, that he would be prosecuted for driving while disqualified, an imprisonable offence. He looked shocked.

After urgently consulting with his interpreter the latter announced that he thought he had only been banned from driving his Porsche.

"I didn't think the ban applied to me driving my children's cars."

ONE TOO MANY

Asked by a Clerkenwell magistrate whether he had anything to say, a Hoxton builder on a drink-driving charge replied, "I've got seven kids and I had one over the eight."

TRIED AND TESTED

Consider the fate of an unfortunate Slough housewife who succeeded in getting breathalysed while taking her driving test.
Having failed it six times before she felt in need of a little liquid fortification before taking her seventh, and although the examiner commented on the smell of alcohol on her breath she assured him she had just taken a medicinal nip to soothe a cold.

Come the emergency stop, however, and she slammed her foot down on the accelerator instead of the brake. Before the examiner could interfere she had smashed into the back of a stationary car.

Unfortunatley it was a police car.

SHUM MISHTAKE

An advertising executive driving North over the Sydney Harbour Bridge saw a Booze Bus and a number of cars lined up with their drivers waiting to be tested. Knowing he'd had too much to drink he drew up short of the police and the queue and sauntered up to the test area.

"Look," he said, "I've just left a party nearby and before I drive I would like to be tested to make sure I'm not over the limit."

Politely he was told that Random Breath Tests were for drivers only and not for conscientious pedestrians. So he returned to his car, started it and decided to risk driving past the Booze Bus. Incredibly he was not asked to pull over.

Relieved, he got home, parked the car in the garage and went to bed. He was woken by a loud knocking on the door. Two large policemen confronted him.

"Are you the owner of car type etc. registration number etc?" he was asked. He admitted he was. "At about 10.00 p.m. last night were you driving North over the Harbour Bridge?" Again he admitted he was.

"And did you stop for some reason short of the Random Breath Test Unit?"

"Yes, I did," he had to admit, surprised they knew so much about his movements.

"Would you mind showing us your car?"

After getting dressed he escortd them to the garage and opened the door. There was the Highway Patrol car he'd driven home the night before.

ACCOUNTING FOR THE ACCOUNTANT

The Japanese know how to nurse a grudge.

Two years after he had been accused of reckless driving by his accountant, and successfully prosecuted, a Japanese businessman filled himself with *sake* and ran him down.

The accountant suffered a broken leg and had to spend two and a half weeks in hospital. His ex-client was given even more time to rest: eighteen months in prison.

SHORT MEASURES

A theatrical dwarf who appeared in court on a drink-driving charge explained, "I'm so short that I couldn't cope with the long drinks, only the shorts."

SHUNOTHER MISHTAKE

A London businessman was speeding home up the M1 in his white Rover late one evening when he was pulled in by the police. Considerably the worse for wear he decided he might stand more of a chance if he got out of his car to greet them. But just as they were about to talk to him Providence intervened. Suddenly two cars smashed into each other on the opposite side of the central reservation. Telling him not to drive so fast the officers rushed across the road. The businessman, thanking every god in the universe, drove home and went to bed.

Several hours later he awoke to hear the front door bell ringing. A policeman was standing there. He wanted to know if the businessman had been driving up the M1 earlier that night and whether he had been stopped by the police. The businessman nervously admitted that he had. The policeman then asked if he could see the businessman's car. There in the garage was a white Rover . . . with a blue light on top.

WHAT PUTS A FIREMAN OUT?

When a Reading fireman was called to a multiple crash on the M4 motorway he ended up scuffling with police after trying to stop them breath-testing a driver. As a result he ended up being reported himself for being drunk while on duty. At a disciplinary hearing he admitted drinking five pints of lager at his station's bar before being called out.

"He's been drinking again."

FEMININE INTUITION

A woman having failed the breathalyser and being driven to the nearest police station in a police car was still sufficiently alert to notice that the constable driving her car behind had no lights on.

"I'd like you to make a note in your report," she told the driver, "that your colleague is currently breaking the law."

On reaching the station she was given a stern warning, and then released.

IGNORING HIS OWN ADVICE

The head of the Dorset police's traffic division was recently sentenced to 28 days in jail, suspended for two years, after admitting driving when he was more than three times over the legal limit.

During Christmas, 1984, he had spearheaded the campaign warning motorists, "If you drink, don't drive."

IT'S ONLY A GAME

In Vancouver there's a particular police inspector who likes playing games. Not tennis, golf or even Trivial Pursuits. His idea of the perfect pastime is to fill a beer glass with 36 slips of paper, each one bearing a specific location. Then, several times a week, he picks one out and sends his policemen to seal off all the exit roads around that location and breathalyse any likely driver.

He calls his game: LOTTO LUSH.

100% PROOF

A Plymouth man who stopped a police car and insisted on taking a breath test to prove to his wife that he was not too drunk to drive ended up being banned for a year.

After his court appearance he revealed that he and his wife had since separated.

A BLOW FOR DRINKING DRIVERS

Legislation is being proposed in Colorado to make first time convicted drunk-drivers fit a Guardian interlock system to their cars as a condition of their probation order.

The device is fitted to the car ignition. Before the car can be started the driver has to blow down a tube. If he is over the limit the car will refuse to start.

NEWS FROM THE COLONIES

Although Hong Kong is still a British colony there is no breathalyser there. In fact, despite its gin and tonic reputation, drinking and driving offences rarely reach the courts. In 1984 there were just 14 prosecutions. In context this marked a dramatic increase of more than 50% over the previous year's figures when there were only nine prosecutions.

One of those concerned a man with the delightful name of A. Mok – who did just that. Intending to engage reverse gear to move away from the Kowloon pier, he instead engaged first gear and sent his car down a flight of stairs into the harbour.

SELF-PUNISHMENT

Another of the rare drink and drive cases from Hong Kong concerns a highly-spirited English polytechnic lecturer who drove into one of the two Cross Harbour tunnels – but the wrong one.

When he saw the on-coming traffic, and realised his mistake, he reversed at great speed, then stopped and tried to execute a three point turn. The car stalled just before he had completed the manoeuvre so he jumped out and attempted to halt the traffic by desperately waving his arms. This he might have succeeded in doing had he put the brake on his car. But he hadn't and with his back turned he didn't notice it slowly rolling towards him. He remains, therefore, one of the few drunken drivers to have been knocked down by his own car.

SWEET AND SOUR

The new Lion Intoximeter introduced in 1984 has been the subject of considerable controversy. It is even said that a Chinese meal can adversely affect its reading. Apparently the intoximeter reacts badly to certain substances used in oriental cooking, particularly aniseed and cumin.

If this is true it means you could leave a Take Away and find they Take Away your licence.

JUST WHEN YOU THOUGHT IT WAS SAFE TO TAKE THE PILL

What stops children may also stop you from driving. Because according to professor Victor Wynn, a specialist at London's St. Mary's Hospital, taking the contraceptive pill can directly affect the level of alcohol in the blood system increasing it by as much as 40%!

That's the bad news. The good news is that women rarely drink and drive – or if they do they don't get caught. Only 1% of convicted drivers are women.

OVER THE TOP ROUND THE SQUARE

A recent traffic jam in central London was not caused by the usual problems of urban congestions. This particular snarl-up was the result of a 'paralytically' drunk woman who drove the wrong way around Trafalgar Square.

Banned for two years for being four times over the legal limit the woman, an EEC translator, said at the time she thought she was in Brussels.

PARTY POLITICS

Dr. Kenneth Kaunda, the president of Zambia and a tee-totaller, is apparently very concerned about the rise of drinking and driving which has claimed the lives of several of his close associates.

At a recent meeting he threatened to resign if excessive drinking continued. Came a voice form the back of the hall: "I'll drink to that."

DRINKING AND DRIVING FOR A LIVING

Three years ago in the North Wales town of Mold, a constable stood in the dock accused of crashing his car while under the influence of alcohol and while on duty. Yet despite the severity of the case the magistrates only fined him £120 and allowed him to keep his licence after they had been told that the constable was under orders to drink as part of an undercover operation.

TWO HEADS ARE BETTER THAN ONE

Two policemen saw a curious sight as they drove along a quiet suburban road just after midnight. A Vauxhall Viva was weaving towards them and they could distinctly make out the head of a man in the driving seat. But just a few inches below was the head of a woman also facing the steering wheel.

The officers did a U-turn and flagged down the car. When they opened the door they found the man in the driving seat with his feet on the control pedals and a woman perched on his lap with both hands on the steering wheel.

Sheepishly, the couple got out of the car and stood on the pavement. There was a distinct smell of drink. The two police officers, however, were posed with a problem. Who was legally the driver of the car: the man or the woman? And which of the two should be breathalysed?

They decided to breathalyse both, and both tests proved positive.

"Don't move; I'll tell him we're Siamese twins."

1872 AND ALL THAT

The Licensing Act of 1872, which is still on the Statute Book, states:

'Any person who is drunk on any highway or any other public place while in charge of any carriage, horse, cattle or steam engine may be apprehended and shall be liable to a penalty not exceeding £10, or at the discretion of the court to imprisonment with or without hard labour for any term not exceeding one month.'

So next time you're found drunk in charge of a cow in a public place don't say you haven't been warned.

ABSENCE MAKES THE CAR GO FURTHER

An unemployed plumber in Preston took a second-hand car for a test drive. Two days later he was stopped in London for speeding and found to be twice over the limit. He also possessed no driving licence.

He told police he was missing his girlfriend who had recently moved South.

CLAMPING DOWN ON DRUNKEN DRIVERS

A celebration turned into a nightmare when Bob Knight returned to where he had left his car to discover it had been clamped.

Such was his rage and level of intoxication that he ignored all the warnings stuck across the windows, got in and attempted to drive off.

The front wheel was immediately torn off and he came to a grinding halt in the middle of the road.

He later tried to persuade the court that in the darkness he hadn't realised his car had been clamped.

THE OLDEST VICTIM

In 1973 a man aged 73 was found going round in circles outside a Tonbridge pub. He was, he said afterwards, confused as to where to go next. According to a passing policeman he was also over the limit.

Uncharitably banning him for three years, local magistrates additionally ordered him to pay £4.20 in costs – at 5p a week.

DISTANT RELATIVES

A Christchurch man, and an ardent racing enthusiast, flew to Melbourne for the annual Cup. After clearing customs and immigration he hired a car and drove into Melbourne.

Having time to kill, he stopped at a bar, and there by chance met a distant cousin who he hadn't seen for years. To celebrate the reunion, champagne was called for and much was consumed. His Melbourne cousin insisted he stay at his house rather than a hotel, and since they still had some time to spare they drove via his house to drop off the Christchurch cousin's luggage.

At the race course even more champagne was called for and, again, much was consumed, especially since the Christchurch man picked an early winner. When the races were over the relative suggested they carried on their celebration at a friend's who was throwing a party.

It was a marvellous party but come midnight the Melbourne cousin had had enough. He told his Christchurch cousin he was going home. "Fine," accepted the latter. "I'll come on later."

By 4.30 a.m. he had also had enough, but then he realised he had no idea where his relative lived. He asked around but the few guests left had never heard of him and there was no sign of the host. In desperation he rang his wife in Christchurch. She, less than pleased at being woken up and suspicious of why her husband was still at a party, didn't know either. Eventually he persuaded her to ring her aunt in Wellington who was closely related to his Melbourne cousin. Half an hour later his wife phoned back with the address.

Now he had the address but he had no idea how to get there. The two remaining guests seemed to have no idea either, and there was still no sign of the host.

Unsteadily he climbed into his car and set off in the hope that he would meet someone who could direct him. Unfortunately, all he met was a police car. They had spotted him weaving across the road and they also quickly spotted he had been drinking. He was breathalysed, found to be way over the limit and arrested.

For more than four hours he was detained at the police station. It didn't help that he was a New Zealander, driving a hired car, but eventually, after a court hearing had been fixed, he was allowed to take a taxi back to his cousin's house. He walked in desperately tired, depressed and hungover.

"You left the party without telling me where you live," he accused his cousin.

His cousin looked amazed. "But I only live next door."

SELF-EMPLOYMENT

Coming soon to the streets of Toronto: coin-operated breathalyser machines.

Why let the police do the job when you can do it yourself?

EVERY DOG HAS HIS DAY

A Northampton lorry driver stopped by police in a routine check of his lorry's roadworthiness was found to be anything but roadworthy himself. He was breathalysed and arrested. So was his passenger: a six year old Great Dane.

On their way to the police station the lorry driver pointed out tht the dog was innocent and couldn't it therefore be dropped off at its home. The police officer driving, being a dog-lover, agreed to make the necessary detour.

It was a detour which saved the lorry driver his licence and probably guaranteed that the police driver would never be kind to a dog again, for having reached the station, the lorry driver argued that he had not been properly arrested and the court agreed with him.

A DRIVING LESSON

A schoolteacher was driving home at three in the morning after a night of consoling an old girlfriend facing a divorce. Since much of the consolation had been of a liquid variety she became a little concerned when, looking in her rear view mirror, she saw what she suspected was a plain clothes police car tailing her.

She increased her speed. So did the car behind. She drove even faster and succeeded in losing her pursuer who had radioed for support. Several other cars attempted to catch her but it was the first one which finally found her again and forced her off the road.

She climbed out of her car genuinely angry and began screaming at the plain clothes policeman that she had never been so frightened in her life. She thought she was being chased by two rapists and how was she supposed to know they were policemen?

Her ploy worked. Not only was she not given a breath test but she was also escorted home.

THE RUNAWAY COACH

A nervous coach driver who was warned that driving conditions were atrocious on the M5 between Bristol and Exeter because of high winds, downed half a bottle of whisky to steady his nerves before setting off.

As a result he kept falling asleep at the wheel, repeatedly switched lanes frequently hitting the kerb in the process, and collided with two cars – one of them a police car. Finally a terrified passenger grabbed the handbrake and ordered him off the coach.

When the police caught up with him he was found to be three times over the legal limit. He was subsequently banned for five years and fined a total of £1,200.

"Shouldn't you have stopped the coach *before* you ordered him off?"

BACCHUS ON THE BYPASS

A group of Surrey estate agents who had managed to introduce lunch to dinner, finally broke up and went off to their respective homes. One drove home taking in the A25 Guildford by-pass which was being repaired at the time. The inner lane had been cordoned off with railway sleepers. But the driver failed to notice this and proceeded to drive over them completely ripping off the undercarriage of his car. The seriousness of the situation began to percolate through his alcoholic haze but he realised there was nothing he could immediately do to rectify it. He also realised how much he had drunk. Getting out he began climbing up the embankment.

About half an hour later, just as he was reching civilisation, and a phone box, he realised he had left his brief case on the front passenger seat. It contained a number of important papers. Swearing, he retraced his footsteps.

It was dark by the time he reached his car and he was still suffering the effects of lunch. He went to open the door.

"Good evening!" a voice boomed out from within. A lesser man might have died from shock. The estate agent reeled back as a policeman climbed out. "We thought you might return, sir," the policeman said holding the brief case "I wonder if you would mind taking a breath test."

THE 1985 TRAFFIC ACT

The former wife of a well-known actor put on a performance herself when she drove into the back of an Arab's car in the West End of London.

In an attempt to avoid the breathalyser she jumped on to the bonnet of her car and pretended she had been knocked over.

POLICE SUPPORT

Police officer in New South Wales are currently voicing anger about possible legislation which would require them to drive drunk drivers home instead of locking them up.

"We'll be buying them drinks next," one officer sarcastically remarked.

END OF THE ARGUMENT

When an Ipswich builder was stopped by police for speeding he immediately started arguing with the officer that he had been travelling below the legal speed limit. The officer was unimpressed. He said the car's speed had been monitored by radar. Still the builder insisted he was innocent and he turned to his wife for support.

But his wife offered him the kind of marital support he could have well done without. Leaning across her husbnd she told the officer, "He's not normally this argumentative. It's just that he's had a few drinks."

MOLOTOV COCKTAIL

Stopped during one of Bombay's rare breaks in its notorious traffic jams, an Indian merchant pulled out a cigarette to steady his nerves. Tragically, the poor man had drunk so much that on going to light his cigarette the alcohol fumes ignited killing him instantly.

THE WORST MAN

It was a romantic, Spring afternoon and the young bride-groom was nervously waiting inside a Highgate church for his bride to arrive, and his best man. The bride appeared looking radiant, arm-in-arm with her father, but there was still no sign of the best man. The vicar and congregation started inspecting their watches and both groom and bride cast each other anxious looks. The screech of a car braking outside signalled the belated arrival of the best man. Red in the face, panting and smelling of booze he mumbled his apologies for being so late and took his place next to his friend. The service commenced.

A few mintues later, he suddenly became panic-stricken. In an urgent whisper he informed the bridegroom he had for-gotten the ring, but living so close he promised it would only take him a moment to get it. Before the bridegroom could react, he shot down the aisle, much to the surprise of the guests, and particularly the bride and vicar.

But he never returned. On his way back to his house he was stopped, breathalysed and arrested.

EVERYONE LOVES A LOVER

Noticing a car parked on a set of double yellow lines with its hazard warning lights flashing, a policeman went to investigate. Inside he found a woman slumped over the steering wheel with a half-empty bottle of whisky lying beside her. The policeman knocked on the window and she eventually responded. He asked her whether she had been drinking.

"Yes, a lot," she replied with a slur. "All I want to do is die."

The policeman asked her for a breath specimen. She simply kept repeating, "I want to die." He had no choice but to charge her with refusing to take a breath test.

But she got off.

"Why? Because Bedford Magistrates ruled that since earlier that night she had split up with her boyfriend she was too upset to take a breath test, and it was a decision the Appeal Court upheld.

"Would you mind blowing into this before you jump, madam?"

LEGLESS (i)

A graphic artist has pleaded that the breath test showing him to be over the limit should be set aside because, as a one-legged man, he has less blood than a person with two legs and the reading was therefore higher.

LEGLESS (ii)

A British road safety chief wants to extend the role of the breathalyser and use it to randomly test drunken pedestrians. She told a medical conference, "They stagger out of pubs and clubs drunk and often end up in the path of a passing car. The driver has no chance."

But if her demand becomes law what kind of sentence would a court pass?

"You're banned from walking for a year. You'll have to drive instead."

WHISKY, WHISKY EVERYWHERE

Late one wet and windy evening two Totness policmen saw a man scrambling up a hillside screaming "Whisky!" His car was parked half on the road and half on the verge with its engine running.

When they investigated further they discovered the man was not calling for fortification but trying to retrieve his dog, a Scotch terrier. It had jumped out when he had stopped for a pee.

Unfortunately, he had also been drinking the liquid version and he ended up being breathalysed.

ONE OF THE BOYS

A police constable who failed a breath test while returning from a day trip to France had no shortage of witnesses.

He was driving a mini-bus full of policemen.

DRUNK IN CHARGE OF AN UNIDENTIFIED OBJECT

The first person to be charged with being drunk whilst driving the Sinclair C5 (remember the C5?) managed to completely confuse the court as to what he was precisely driving, or riding.

At 4 a.m. he was spotted pedalling a C5 along the pavement because having just won it in a raffle he didn't know how to connect the battery. Realising he'd been seen he took to the road where he was stopped by a police car.

The police eventually tried to prosecute him on the grounds that he was riding a tricycle whilst unfit through drink, and quoted as a precedent a 1917 case of an invalid found drunk in charge of a bathchair. But the magistrate was unimpressed. He told the police solicitor he, "was in difficulties," and dimissed the case.

"Not that I blame you, sir, I'd want a drink before I got in one of those things."

TIME GENTLEMAN, PLEASE

In order to give some of their officers a wider experience, the Bodmin Police Force instigated a two week experiment. The two officers from the small village of St. Merryn were posted to the town of Wadebridge, another two from Wadebridge to the city of Bodmin, and a further two from Bodmin were sent to look after St. Merryn.

No-one, however, felt it necessary to inform one of the village pub's most loyal and dedicated regulars, known to all as Gentleman Jim, of this temporary change in policing.

Jim had acquired his prefix because of his aristocratic accent and pretentions, and rarely a night passed without him making an appearance at the Farmer's Arms. Rarely a night also passed without Gentleman Jim exceeding the limit – both his own and the hours the pub was legally supposed to keep.

Shortly after the new policing arrangements had taken effect Gentleman Jim staggered across the pub's car park to begin his five mile drive home. It was nearly 1 a.m. As he left the village he saw the local police car approaching him. It was a vision which caused him little concern. He knew the two officers well and made a habit of playing golf with one of them at least once a month. He gave them a friendly flash of his headlights.

The two Bodmin officers were unused to such acts of rural familiarity. From their point of view, here was a man driving his Rover somewhat uncertainly and certainly too fast, in the middle of the night, and who for no apparent reason, suddenly decided to blind them with his headlights. They in turn decided to investigate.

Four months later Gentlemam Jim ceased to be a regular at the Farmer's Arms.

DEJA VU

Late one night in New Zealand a Wellington police car passed a man sleeping in his car. They woke him up and unaware he'd been drinking told him to drive home.

Surprised by their attitude, but not wishing to discuss the matter for fear of being breathalysed, he did as they requested. But before he managed to reach his home he was stopped by a second police car whose occupants were more attentive. They immediately noticed he had been drinking, and despite his protests, asked him to take a breath test.

The reading was just marginally over the limit. The police decided to exercise their discretion. They told him to take a short nap and then he should be OK to drive.

"FILL ME UP PLEASE, LANDLORD"

A Kerry man unimpressed by the car manufacturers' latest models decided to design and build his own. Dismissing such accessories as chrome strips, mock leather upholstery, thick fitted carpet and shock absorbers as being purely cosmetic, his first creation looked like something designed by Heath Robinson during an LSD trip. On its inaugural run, it managed the grand distance of a hundred yards before grinding to a flaming halt.

But being a Kerry man he persevered...and persevered. After nearly a year his unique creation was potentially capable of covering the vital ground between his home and his local hostelry. It was a potential he realised one Autumn morning, and which provoked a considerable celebration on arrival.

It was while returning several hours later that his mobile masterpiece grabbed the attention of the local constable. Knowing the driver well, and aware of his plans to challenge the supremacy of Ford, he was still amazed to see the result. He beckoned for the man to stop, which eventually he did after some initial difficulty.

With a mixture of amusement and awe the constable inspected the outside then looked inside. The proud and happy driver was sitting on a modified kitchen chair. It was the vehicle's only seat. Next to him on the wooden floor was a crate of Guinness.

"Don't tell me," the constable said with heavy irony, "This here vehicle runs on Guinness."

"If it does," came the driver's equally ironic response, "then I've been drinking petrol."

TOO KEEN TO STOP

A Cape Town imbiber, his thoughts elsewhere, suddenly noticed a police car flashing him from behind. Unfortunately he over-reacted and breaked too suddenly. Still flashing, the police car smashed into his rear. Worse still, a third car smashed into the back of the police car.

THE BREATHLESS GARDENER

On reaching Dartford police station, Mrs. Gill Reeves found she was unable to produce a second breath test. Being only 4' 8" tall and weighing just over seven stone she had a considerably reduced lung capacity.

While police waited for her to get her breath back she occupied the time taking cuttings from their plants at the station.

BLIND OR DRUNK? (i)

The singer Stevie Wonder has now joined the growing campaign to put an end to drunken driving among teenagers. Having already released a single called "Don't Drive Drunk," he has now appeared in a poster beneath the headline, "Before I'll ride with a drunk, I'll drive myself."

BLIND OR DRUNK? (ii)

Arrested for careless driving on the Chesapeake Turnpike, Mr. Dan Morgan of Portsmouth, Virginia said, "My friend and I had been to a party where he got drunk. When the time came to go home we discussed the matter and decided it was safer for me to take the wheel even though I am completely blind."

"I've had rather a lot to drink so I thought I'd better let him drive."

SAMPLING THE PRODUCT

Every year there is a race to see who can bring the first bottles of Beaujolais Nouveau into Britain. But for two French lorry drivers bringing the wine in, the only race was to see which of them could drink the most in transit.

By the time they reached Dover they were both nearly three times over the legal limit. One literally fell out of the lorry at customs. The other couldn't even get that far. He'd fallen asleep in his cab shortly after boarding the ferry.

INFLATION

After the breathalyser's first year in business there had been 7,000 successful convictions. At the end of 1983, during a twelve month period, over 80,000 motorists had been convicted.

That's a 1200% increase – just slightly more than the price of a pint had increased over the same period.

ALL'S WELL THAT ENDS WELL

Like the past, they do things differently in the Cambrian mountains of Wales and when one of its sparse population was stopped late at night and asked to take a breath test he resorted to an age-old custom to remedy the situation. He threatened to curse the arresting officer.

Now the officer being young and new to the region was a little apprehensive about forcing the issue, especially once the wild-eyed local had launched into muttering his Celtic incantations of doom and dismay and waving his arms around in an alarming fashion. His companion, however, being older and wiser, intervened. Curse or no curse, he warned the Welsh Wizard that unless he hurried up and took a breath test he would be arrested for threatening a police officer.

The end of the story? Not quite. For should you ever find yourself driving along the B4518 between Rhayader and Llanidloes look out for a couple of tall stones of the left hand side of the road. In the half-light of dusk they bear an uncanny likeness to two frozen policemen.

Acknowledgements

In trying to track down stories from the UK and abroad I was greatly assisted by the co-operation of numerous embassies in London, foreign newspaper libraries, the British Library at Collindale and Holborn Library.

I would also like to thank the following individuals for providing me with further stories, either directly or indirectly. Les Evans, Geoff Wild, Arthur Sturgess, John Ingham, Sam Jackman, David Humphreys, Richard Bemaid and a host of drinking companions.

Particular thanks to Susanna Scott-Gall who helped with the research, and to Rothes Currie who unearthed several stories and kindly typed the final result.

Finally, a word of thanks to the Metropolitan Police. Had they not breathalysed me I would never have had the idea in the first place.